My cat is ignoring me!?

First published in Great Britain
in 2009 by Spruce, an imprint of
Octopus Publishing Group Ltd
Carmelite House
50 Victoria Embankment
London EC4Y 0DZ
www.octopusbooks.co.uk

An Hachette UK Company
www.hachette.co.uk

The authorized representative
in the EEA is Hachette
Ireland, 8 Castlecourt Centre,
Dublin 15, D15 XTP3, Ireland
(email: info@hbgi.ie)

This edition published
in 2026 by Hamlyn

Text copyright © Peter
Wedderburn 2009, 2026

Illustration copyright ©
Per José Karlén 2009, 2026

Distributed in the US by
Hachette Book Group
1290 Avenue of the Americas,
4th and 5th Floors
New York, NY 10104

Distributed in Canada by
Canadian Manda Group
664 Annette St., Toronto,
Ontario, Canada M6S 2C8

All rights reserved. No part of
this work may be reproduced
or utilized in any form or by any
means, electronic or mechanical,
including photocopying,
recording or by any information
storage and retrieval system,
without the prior written
permission of the publisher.

Peter Wedderburn asserts the
moral right to be identified
as the author of this work.

ISBN: 978-0-60064-004-2
eISBN: 978-0-60064-005-9

A CIP catalogue record for
this book is available from
the British Library.

Printed and bound in China.

10 9 8 7 6 5 4 3 2 1

Publisher: Lucy Pessell
Senior Editor: Tim Leng
Designer: Isobel Platt
Assistant Editor: Samina Rahman
Production Manager:
Caroline Alberti

MIX
Paper | Supporting
responsible forestry
FSC® C144853

Peter Wedderburn

Illustrated by Per José Karlén

My cat is ignoring me!?

Practical advice for cat lovers

Contents

Introduction 8

Pick of the litter 10
- How do I choose a happy healthy cat?
- Boy or girl? Does it make any difference?
- Long hair or short?
- What about a rescue cat?
- What sort of cat carrier is the best?
- How should I welcome them into their new home?
- Home alone? Or is happiness a crowd of cats?

Kitty Litter And Cat Naps 22
- Indoors or outdoors? Where will they be happiest?
- Should I give my cat their own key so that they can let themselves in at night?
- Their place or mine? Where should they sleep?
- Choosing their bathroom suite: what type of litter tray is best?
- What type of litter material will they prefer?
- They left a 'number two' in my (now ex-) partner's shoe. Why?

Fat cats and picky pets 32
- Why does my cat insist on drinking from the toilet?
- What type of food bowl will my cat prefer?
- Junk food or haute cuisine? Should I read the cat food label?

- Caviar? Oysters? What food can I give my cat to make them love me?
- Crunchy or juicy? Dry food or tins and sachets?
- I think my cat is too fat. How can I break this to them gently?
- How can I keep their teeth clean without making them hate me?

Hissy fits 46

- I know a dog is a 'lesser' being, but could they like each other?
- My cat ignores me all the time. How can I get their attention?
- I know my cat's in a mood, but why do they have to pee on my sofa?
- My cat gets all cuddly, then suddenly bites me!
- My cat wants to sit on the table. How can I teach them not to (nicely)?
- My cat hates car journeys. How can I cheer them up on trips?
- What is my cat thinking?
- My cat drags live prey through the cat flap. Help!
- What's wrong with the scratching post I bought my cat?
- My cat is being bullied by the next-door cat. What can I do?
- My cat is in a mood because I'm going on holiday. What shall I do with them?

Feline fun 66
- They keep bringing their friends around. How can I keep
- them out?
- My cat looks bored. How can I make their home more interesting?
- How about giving my cat a gentle massage? Any tips?
- How can I make a pedicure more fun for my cat?
- Would the sweet scent of aromatherapy oils help my cat to relax?
- They don't like their toy mouse. Any ideas for better play objects?
- How can I help them to have a long life, as well as a happy one?
- Would my cat be happier if they had their own family?

Looking after their nine lives 78
- How can I make my cat let me groom them?
- My cat hates the vet. Do I need to take them there?
- How do I choose a good cat vet?
- The vet costs a fortune. Any cheap options?
- Why should I give them a worm dose?
- I think it hurts when they eat. Could they have toothache?
- My cat isn't itching, but could fleas be making them miserable?
- My cat hates injections. Do they really need those vaccines?
- I want them to be fit. What can I do?
- My cat doesn't want to wear their collar. Do they have to?
- Give them tablets? You must be joking!

About the author 95

Introduction

Cats are very different to human-loving, owner-pleasing dogs. Cats are independent creatures who seem only ever to do their own thing. In feline current jargon, cats don't even have owners: they have 'guardians' with whom they choose to share a home.

Cats can come across as unappreciative of their human consorts, and many people wonder what they could do to make their cats reciprocate with a little more affection and attention. Are there any 'tricks of the trade' that could help to make an aloof, arrogant feline into a cuddly, affectionate cat?

If your cat is already a people-loving puss, you may still wonder if you are catering properly to their needs. How can you be sure that you are allowing them to live the healthiest and happiest way of life?

There are numerous information sources dedicated to cat care, but cat owners often have simple questions that remain unanswered. This book aims to resolve some of those queries, with practical, uncomplicated advice.

This volume contains 50 ways to ensure you are giving your cat the best possible lifestyle, and includes tips on how to make your cat a little more appreciative of their human companions. Keeping a cat is an enjoyable and rewarding experience, or should be. After reading this book, you will be able to improve the cat-human relationship in your home, so that it IS more fun - for both of you.

Chapter 1
Pick of the litter

How do I choose a happy healthy cat?

Simple: choose a happy healthy cat in the first place. As tear-jerking as a snivelly animal with runny eyes and waxy ears is, health problems, such as cat flu viral infections, can be lifelong issues, which is why it's crucial that your cat's engine purrs from the word go. Deny every instinct that tells you that the hissing, snarling kitten in the corner can be tamed: it can't.

Most humans end up like our parents and so do cats. It's a genetic thing, so it's worth meeting the parents for a dosage of home truths. Tomcats, however, tend to be the worst form of absentee fathers, so don't hold too much hope in meeting dad. Plus, the old Jesuit saying, 'Show me the kitten [boy] at seven weeks old and I will show you the cat [man]', rings true. A calm, relaxed kitten is most likely to turn into a friendly, easy-going adult cat.

Of course, there are exceptions – the sofa-shredding kitten that transforms into a purring lap-cat and the half-wild kitten that becomes a calm, contented adult – and sometimes your heartstrings will tug to the extent that you choose an animal regardless of its health and nature. But as a rule of thumb, go for the cute, healthy-looking cat that will warm your heart and your sofa for years to come.

Boy or girl? Does it make any difference?

What is sex when it comes to sparkling personality? Seeing as most cats are neutered before maturity anyway, you'll be choosing on the assets of their character, rather than their gender. Both male and female cats can be wonderful companions, and both sexes also can be cantankerous bullies. If you already have a cat, avoid the all-girls-school social stresses by having a mix of sexes to break up the tension.

Also, it's a little cheaper to have male cats neutered than females, but the saving is pennies in your pocket. The difference will buy you a couple of big bags of cat food, not a yacht.

Long hair or short?

If only we humans could master tongue grooming, hair appointments would be a thing of the past. Self-grooming is enough for shorthaired cats to maintain shiny, tangle-free coats without the need for a frenzy of shampoos and hairbrushes. Longhaired cats, however, especially pure-breeds like Persians, will need your help in the more difficult-to-lick places such as behind the ears and under the tail. If you want the exotic beauty of a longhaired cat, be prepared to make good friends with the brush and comb, or grit your teeth and bear paying a vet or groomer to clip off matted fur.

Fur balls, a common cause of vomiting in the cat world, are less common in shorthaired cats, so let your yukkiness tolerance influence your decision.

Finally, how house-proud are you? Hairier cat – hairier carpet. A simple equation.

What about a rescue cat?

Claim your good-citizen badge by choosing the homeless moggy, but go carefully! Albert Einstein said, 'Men marry women with the hope they will never change. Women marry men with the hope they will change. Invariably they are both disappointed.' Cats are more like men than women: don't assume their personalities will change dramatically.

Cats can live for twenty years or more, so anticipate having to share your life with this creature for a big chunk of it. Avoid the skittish, bad-tempered variety that will take your hand off when you demand a space in your own bed.

What sort of cat carrier is the best?

Cats lounge: they'll airport lounge, cocktail lounge and 'your' lounge. But journeys involve little to no lounging and invariably lead to either the vet or the cattery – at the prospect of an injection you'd be equally difficult to stuff into a box. That said, you can make travel less stressful by choosing a cat-friendly carrier. It needs to be big enough so they can stand up and turn around; should be designed so they can see out without feeling completely exposed to the world (put a blanket over the carrier if there are wide open gaps); and ensure the door catches are solid and there is no way they can escape. There are wire cages, plastic carriers and fabric hold-all types, and you can go fancy, glitzy or plain. Chances are, although you've gone to all this trouble, your cat is having none of it.

How should I welcome them into their new home?

Time to put in your cat eyes. Have you got high-up resting places (from which your cat's sense of superiority can be satisfied), hiding places (cats like to have their own secret moments), scratching posts (nail filing is not a luxury in the cat world), a cosy bed (electric heating pads are a MUST for the 21st-century moggie), and a few interesting toys? Also, install a plug-in Feliway diffuser, which fills the air with soothing pheromones, so that when your cat walks in, they'll have an immediate sense of coming home. Pheromones are the feline equivalent of wafts of freshly baked bread or freshly ground coffee.

Home alone?
Or is happiness
a crowd of cats?

Toes attacked at breakfast by an attention-seeking kitten? Then try getting them a small, furry, feline playmate. Many cats end up as best buddies, but the wrong mix of personalities can be a less than fun experience. It only takes a few cats streaking past you in terror or fury, and some smelly damp patches of urine on curtains and carpets, for you to long for the days of solo puss. My own rule of thumb is 'no more than three', unless your budget can stretch to frequent visits to the dry cleaner and sessions with the cat psychologist.

Chapter 2
Kitty litter and cat naps

Indoors or outdoors? Where will they be happiest?

Car accidents? Predators? Is your cat's safety keeping you awake at night? Indoor cats may be safer, but outdoor cats can prowl about to their heart's content, which they LOVE to do. Make a compromise. In the daylight they may go outside, with the proviso that the personalized cat flap will let them in if they get cold, wet or tired. But at night, the time when most car accidents and cat fights occur, the cat flap will not open. Your house, your rules.

Should I give my cat their own key so that they can let themselves in at night?

There will be no shimmying up or down the drainpipes and no jumping in and out of windows. With a microchip cat flap, such as a PetSafe cat flap, you control their comings and goings. For those of you with a large feline family or cat-loving disposition, it can be set to accept up to twelve different microchip numbers and you can set a curfew. The cat flap automatically detects light levels, so you can make sure that your cats are safely kept inside during the hours of darkness. See www.petsafe.com for more information.

Their place or mine? Where should they sleep?

A cat will, no matter the obstacles in their path, always find the most comfy, coziest bed. It's a sixth sense.

Another place they LOVE is high-up places where they can lazily survey the room by simply lifting their heads, and their preference is your duvet. You, however, may not enjoy them snoring and snuffling or being woken by a sudden weight on your chest as they reposition themselves for extra warmth.

Create an alternative. In a high-up spot, place a deep-pile, sheepskin-type fleece blanket with a plug-in electric heat pad beneath it. Plug in a Feliway diffuser beside it and suddenly your own bed won't seem quite so appealing to a cat.

Choosing their bathroom suite: what type of litter tray is best?

The three most important aspects of litter trays are size, depth and roof. If you get these wrong, your cat may decide to choose a bathroom location elsewhere in your home.

The more space they have the less likely it is they will go elsewhere, so choose as big a tray as you can fit comfortably into their bathroom area. Be practical when it comes to the depth, too. Spillage is definitely unwanted, but a kitten or arthritic granny-cat can't always clamber over the high sides easily; and just because you panic whenever you've forgotten to lock the bathroom door doesn't mean your cat craves privacy also. Covered litter trays can cause claustrophobia, so remove the cat-flap door, so they feel less shut-in.

What type of litter material will they prefer?

Cat litter: used by cats, chosen by humans. You may prefer the de-odourized, easy-clean, flushable version, but if your cat doesn't like it your carpet and your nerves will be the ones to suffer. More important than choosing something exotic is clean litter material, so change it often. Start off with the type that your kitten or cat is already used to, then make any changes gradually. That funny stain on the bathmat will be a tell-tale sign of their reaction to your purchase.

They left a 'number two' in my (now ex-) partner's shoe. Why?

You feel stressed by it? Imagine how stressed your cat must have been to embark upon such an extreme endeavour. It may have been a one-off, but if it happens repeatedly, there must be something making them feel ill-at-ease in their normal bathroom area. Try some new litter trays and new litter materials, but if it continues, professional advice is definitely called for. Partners may not always be replaceable.

Chapter 3
Fat cats and picky pets

Why does my cat insist on drinking from the toilet?

Here comes the science: fresh water from the tap contains chlorine, which dissipates when water is left standing. This means your cat finds toilet water delicious. However, the inevitable moment when they fall in should motivate you to discourage them choosing this source of hydration. Keep the toilet lid closed and try giving your cat filtered, boiled (and cooled) or bottled water in their bowl. They won't like water by their food bowl, so have a few small bowls dotted about the house. Better again, get a cat fountain, which supplies trickling, filtered water continually. They'll be charmed.

What type of food bowl will my cat prefer?

Plastic is far from fantastic. Ceramic or stainless steel bowls don't become scratched and grimy over time and prevent possible allergic skin reactions. Dinner-excited cats tend to push their plates around, so to stop food spillages choose a bowl with a rim, rather than a flat plate. Also, if you're feeding dry food, don't leave a small mountain of food piled in a bowl. Hide small amounts of kibble around the house instead, so that your cat has to hunt for them. Cats enjoy the challenge and the tasty reward; plus it keeps their brain cells energized.

Junk food or haute cuisine? Should I read the cat food label?

Decoding the jargon on the ingredients label can be a tricky task. 'Meat and animal derivatives' can describe any meat or animal by-product, without specifying what it is or even which species it comes from. This allows manufacturers to hide the not-so-impressive ingredients, and it enables them to change the protein source with every batch without having to change the label. There are over 4,000 permitted chemical additives that can be used in pet food without individually naming them, and plenty of these additives are know to cause hyperactivity in children. Imagine what they are doing to poor puss! Whenever you can, choose more natural foods with as few artificial additives as possible.

Caviar? Oysters? What food can I give my cat to make them love me?

Money can't buy you love, but it can buy very expensive, good-quality cat food. You cat would wear diamonds if they could, so you know not to scrimp on a cheap alternative – cheaper foods equal cheaper ingredients. Apply the maxim 'you are what you eat'. Cats on a top-quality diet ooze good health, so give them a month or two for the premium diet to kick in.

Crunchy or juicy? Dry food or tins and sachets?

Shake up the boring world of cat food with a combination of the moist and dry. Moist food (tins and sachets) tends to be enjoyed more than dry food by cats, and is more like a 'natural' cat diet with high levels of protein and moisture and low levels of carbohydrate. But dry foods are very convenient, less smelly, less likely to go off and they can help to keep a cat's teeth healthy. Try a small moist meal once or twice daily, supplemented with some dry food. At different times in your cat's life, for different reasons, you may want to give more or less of either moist or dry food, but it's best if they are familiar with both.

I think my cat is too fat. How can I break this to them gently?

Shift the responsibility. Get the vet to weigh them at their annual check up, and they can break the news. As you console them afterwards, tell them that about one in four cats is overweight, so they're not alone. The vet will offer them some simple ways to fight the flab. The usual rules of fewer calories, more exercise can be made to sound more palatable if you talk about 'tasty, light food and more play'. It's important that they stay around their ideal weight, because as in humans, obesity is linked with health complications that you could both do without, including arthritis, heart disease and diabetes.

How can I keep their teeth clean without making them hate me?

Just like you, your cat's fangs need regular brushing. However, the odds of them allowing you to stick a strange plastic, bristly object into their mouth on even one occasion, never mind after every meal, are not good. If a kitten has been trained into tooth brushing from an early age, then it may be a possibility, but for most cats, you'll need hypnosis or total sedation. Alternatively, try the next best thing: special prescription-only dry diets, available from vets, that simulate natural abrasive chewing.

Chapter 4
Hissy fits

I know a dog is a 'lesser' being, but could they like each other?

Cat and dog might be mortal enemies, but there are a few tricks to bring out the white flag. Starting with a chilled-out cat and a calm, obedient dog can be key to a happy menagerie, and catching them while one, but ideally both, is young is also a great start to the peacekeeping process.

The wide-eyed innocence of puppies and kittens makes them difficult for any creature to dislike strongly, so place one of the two in a large wire mesh cage at the start, preventing either from lashing out until they've grown accustomed to one another. Prolonged time in each other's company may be enough to forge a truce, but, as with humans, it's impossible to force a friendship.

My cat ignores me all the time. How can I get their attention?

Cats are proud creatures, so be prepared to indulge them. They're far too smart to be won over by you playing hard to get, so swallow your pride and do some good, old-fashioned sucking up. Get a new toy and play games with them; get down on your knees to have a chat while they eat their dinner; and when they are sleeping, sit beside them and pet them. Just as long as no one sees you making a fool of yourself, it will work out well.

I know my cat's in a mood, but why do they have to pee on my sofa?

Feline shrinks have named this phenomenon 'inappropriate elimination'. There are many causes, but stress of some kind is often involved. Whether there is a new cat bully living nearby, your new girlfriend in their sofa space, or a new type of litter in your cat's tray, something is rubbing their fur up the wrong way. Clean up the piddled area properly and visit your vet sooner rather than later before a one-off accident becomes a life-long habit.

Cleaning up piddled patches:
1. Clean up with a warm, mild solution of biological washing powder.
2. Rinse with warm water.
3. Apply a spray of surgical spirit (do a patch test first to make sure that the surface will not be damaged).
4. Dab the surface dry.
5. Spray on Feliway, a bottled pheromone that will make your cat less keen to go back to the same place, as it will smell so pleasant to them.

My cat gets all cuddly, then suddenly bites me!

Swishing tail? Ears pinned back? Looks like Dr Jekyll, yes? Wrong. It's Mr Hyde. They're peeved and about to sink their teeth into your forearm. Be careful with body language. Some cats aren't into smothering, and would much prefer you to play with them than give them cuddles. Short periods of petting are best, and if your cat tenses up, move away. They'll curl up on your lap when they're ready. If it's not working out, they need to see a shrink.

My cat wants to sit on the table. How can I teach them not to (nicely)?

You sit at the table, so why shouldn't your cat? It has a fabulous vista, often accompanied by a selection of delicious snacks, reading materials and a warm computer keyboard.

Be crafty. Make the table less fun. Cut out a large piece of card and stick double-sided tape to it in a grid-like pattern, leaving the sticky side up. When you go out, leave the card on the table. If your cat does climb onto the table, they will find it a distinctly unpleasant experience.

My cat hates car journeys. How can I cheer them up on trips?

They're caterwauling, the kids are shrieking 'Are we there yet?' and you've only just left home. They will never be into life's journeys, but you can make them a little comfier for them. Choose as big a cat carrier as you can, so that they have plenty of space, and include a litter tray if possible. Make sure they won't be hungry, and travel at night, if possible, as they are more likely to sleep. Give them some familiar bedding and perhaps an old sweatshirt of your own to snuggle into. Spray some Feliway pheromones into their cage before you leave, then top them up every few hours to give them an ongoing sense of comfort.

What is my cat thinking?

Look into their eyes and ask them. They will look back at you with their sphinx-like gaze and the mystery will remain. It is part of the charm of cats – the inscrutability. Do they know something we don't know? Is there some hidden depth? Is something going on beyond the knowledge of simple humans, on a different level altogether? Or are they just wondering what's for supper and which bed will be the most warm and comfy?

My cat drags live prey through the cat flap. Help!

Cute, fluffy cat? Or mean, blood-thirsty predator? They brings their prey home with them because it is a safe place to finish them off and eat them at they're leisure. They won't judge you in any way for whatever you do with the prey. Do as you wish: rescue the poor wee creature if you can; finish it off if it is badly injured or just shut the door and leave them to it. Nature is tough, and cats are part of it.

What's wrong with the scratching post I bought my cat?

There's a trail of shredded fabric leading from your couch back to a peacefully purring pussycat. Do you wring their neck or realize that their scratching post does not live up to the desirability of the sofa when it comes to using their nails? Try finding them a similar surface to the sofa or some corrugated cardboard to cover the scratching post, and make sure the post is tall enough for them to scratch at full stretch. Perhaps even dangle some toys off it and sprinkle catnip around the base to make it more attractive than the sofa.

My cat is being bullied by the next-door cat. What can I do?

Run Forrest run! Scaredy cats can't be trained into superheroes, so aiding their swift getaway is your smartest option. Give your cat sneaky escape routes, such as a microchipped cat flap, so they can rush inside unpursued. Plan some stepped ledges around the garden to make it more difficult for them to be cornered and give them plenty of toys indoors so that they won't get bored inside. If the next-door cat continues to be beastly, negotiate to 'time share' the two cats. Agree set days to keep each of your cats indoors, so that your cat can enjoy time outside in the knowledge that Top Cat is temporarily locked up.

My cat is in a mood because I'm going on holiday. What shall I do with them?

Boarding cattery or house sitter? Some catteries are genuinely five-star establishments, with piped music, heated beds and pheromone-infused air conditioning. If you can book your cat into a place like this, they will enjoy their holiday as much as you enjoy yours. But do your research. There are also plenty of poor-quality catteries that are best avoided. Many cats prefer to stay at home where they can spread out luxuriously in their new-found independence, over every bed, sofa and floor, with a house sitter either in residence or visiting regularly. This works especially well if there's three or more animals, and it can also be cheaper.

Chapter 5
Feline fun

They keep bringing their friends around. How can I keep them out?

There's a mob of cats inhabiting your living room and what can you do? Chances are they're poor company and have antisocial bathroom habits. Time to employ a bouncer in the form of an automated, magnetic cat flap (see page 26) that only your cat's collar can open. Or go for the cat flaps that will only admit cats implanted with nominated microchip numbers. You can set it up to allow them to bring their well-behaved friends home, while excluding those from less salubrious backgrounds.

My cat looks bored. How can I make their home more interesting?

Take a walk on the wild side. Does your home give them the chance to indulge the wild animal inside them? Are there high surfaces to jump onto and obstacle-course style activities? Can they gaze out of the window with an air of superiority? Visit the International Cat Care website at www.icatcare.org for lots more tips on making a cat-friendly home.

How about giving my cat a gentle massage? Any tips?

Do you enjoy stroking, kneading and 'passive touch'? So does puss. That's why we so instinctively stroke cats. There are multiple books available on pet massage therapy, but trial and error is probably the best way of finding out what suits your own feline friend. Gently squeezing the ear tip between a finger and thumb is very soothing for some cats, but others find it intensely irritating. Many cats are expert masseurs themselves – lying on their owners, kneading their paws up and down.

How can I make a pedicure more fun for my cat?

I'm sure your pedicures don't involve having the ends of your toes squeezed with a sharp metal tool, and if they do, perhaps you should consider changing beautician. Nail clipping can be stressful for cats, so it's important to get them used to being held firmly from kittenhood onwards. Gently squeeze their feet, as if you are shaking their paws, as part of this firm handling. Only when your cat is used to this type of close physical contact should you attempt nail clipping. Remember, they can sense your hesitance and will fight tooth and nail to get away. If in doubt, ask your local vet nurse to do it.

Would the sweet scent of aromatherapy oils help my cat to relax?

Danger! A cat's metabolism works very differently to yours and they lack some enzymes needed for processing common compounds present in some herbs and plants. Remember, too, that their sense of smell is much more sensitive than yours, so a scent that is pleasant to you may be overpowering to them. The safest type of 'aromatherapy' would be to use pheromones – natural, odourless (to humans) chemicals that make animals feel comforted. You can buy cat pheromones, called Feliway, as a spray and as a plug-in vapourizer for a room. You won't notice a pleasant smell (or any smell at all), but your cat will feel happily de-stressed.

They don't like their toy mouse. Any ideas for better play objects?

Mouse, schmouse. Who cares? Certainly not your cat. They're vastly more intelligent than you think, so you'll need to get creative. Fur. Feathers. Leather. Grass. Choose materials that stimulate their natural prey – dangly, stringy toys laced with catnip are much more exciting. Let them chase the bright point from a laser pointer, just don't frustrate them as they can never catch it. To prevent this, place that boring toy mouse under a chair or settee and end the game by directing the pointer at it. They can then grab the mouse and take it away with them, with a sense that they have 'won'.

How can I help them to have a long life, as well as a happy one?

There's no feline elixir of life. Cats can live into their twenties, but there's no guarantee. Feed them the best diet that you can afford and, as they age, give them more moist food to ensure they have a high level of water consumption, which is better for their kidneys. Also, create for them a stress-free, cat-friendly environment. Focus on them from time to time, noticing subtleties like how much water they drink and how fast they breathe. Take them to the vet at least once a year for a physical check-over and perhaps for urine and blood tests. Remember that one human year is seven cat years, so things can change quite rapidly for them compared to a human.

Would my cat be happier if they had their own family?

If you have heard cats procreating in the garden, you will realize that it does not sound like much fun. The process of kittening is not as enjoyable as chasing a laser pointer light across the carpet. And a horde of young kittens hanging off your mammary glands is much harder work than snoozing alone in a pool of warm sunshine. I am quite sure that if they could, your cat would thank you for having them spayed at the recommended age of around four months.

Chapter 6

Looking after their nine lives

How can I make my cat let me groom them?

It is their body, not yours, so cooperation is vital for what can end up as a losing battle. Get cats used to grooming from kittenhood. A once-weekly comb and brush is a simple routine that takes only a few minutes, and it performs a double function of getting your cat used to regular contact with a brush, while removing small knots and mats before they take on a Rastafarian dreadlock style. Leave it too late and the matted fur may be too dense to remove with a comb, and your cat may refuse to allow you anywhere near them with a grooming implement anyway. If this happens, you then need to revert to Plan V – a visit to the vet for the removal of matted fur with electric clippers under sedation. Such drastic action should be enough to convert them to regular grooming.

My cat hates the vet. Do I need to take them there?

A healthy cat is a happy cat. Ideally, their visits to the vet should be kept to a minimum, but they do need their once-yearly check-up. Cats can be clever at hiding problems that need treatment such as sore teeth and irregular heartbeats. Your vet will weigh them, give a thorough physical once-over, administer any necessary vaccinations and parasite control, and listen to your tales of their idiosyncrasies. The annual bundling of the cat into the clinic should be enough to prevent further visits during the year, even if their sharp-clawed resistance might suggest that it's more hassle than it's worth.

How do I choose a good cat vet?

The best way to choose a cat vet is by word of mouth, but you should do a trial visit (without cat) to have a look for yourself. Does the clinic look presentable? Is there handy car parking, so you don't have far to carry your stressed-out cat? Is the waiting room 'cat only', or at least is there some way of keeping noisy dogs out of the way of anxious cats? Are the reception staff friendly people who genuinely like cats? How long are the appointments? And when you eventually take your cat, if they strongly dislike the vet, choose another vet, even within the same practice, and if they dislikes all vets, at least choose one that YOU like.

The vet costs a fortune. Any cheap options?

Simple answer: no! Cheap options result in consequences like amputation instead of fixing a broken leg, or euthanasia instead of an appointment with a pet counsellor. A much better answer is to budget for high-quality vet care from the start by taking out a pet insurance policy from kittenhood onwards. If you are genuinely hard-up and cannot afford insurance, the animal charities, such as the https://icatcare.org and the Blue Cross, do offer good-quality vet care at an affordable price on a means-tested basis.

Why should I give them a worm dose?

Hold your stomach...kittens get roundworms from their mother's milk and older cats get worms of various types from hunting prey and from nibbling fleas that they find in their coat. For the sake of both human and cat health, regular worm doses need to be given. Every three months is the average for adult cats, but this does depend on factors like the area where you live, how much hunting they does and their contact with other animals. Remember, spot-on wormers mean you no longer have to struggle to ram a golf-ball sized tablet down their throat.

I think it hurts when they eat. Could they have toothache?

Cats tend to suffer from the type of toothache that hurts when the tooth is touched, rather than constant throbbing pain. So if you think it hurts them to eat, you could be right. Take them to the vet, who will be able to tell from looking at their teeth (and possibly using a delicately placed probe). Dentists have tried using fillings to fix holes caused by decay in cat teeth, but they tend to fall out. The best answer is simple extraction of painful, diseased teeth. A tooth can't hurt the cat when it's in the waste bin, and the tooth socket soon heals over to become part of a very functional, comfortable and healthy mouth.

My cat isn't itching, but could fleas be making them miserable?

Even the cleanest, most pampered cat can pick up fleas, whether by being close to other cats or just by walking past a place where another cat has been sitting. Fleas make some cats itch furiously, but other, non-allergic, cats can be crawling with fleas without a single scratch. A once-monthly, anti-flea drop from your vet is the safest way to prevent any flea-related issues. Just don't insult your cat by telling them why you are squeezing that vial between their shoulder blades. Like humans, cats sometimes have the mistaken perception that only street moggies get fleas.

My cat hates injections. Do they really need those vaccines?

Even the scientists are out on this one. In recent years evidence has suggested that some modern cat vaccines may last for three years or more, but the product licences are still based on immunity studies of only one year's duration. Most vets still suggest once-yearly vaccines, to be on the safe side. The frequency of vaccination for any cat should be approached on an individual basis, considering genuine risks and needs. Talk to your vet, but make sure your cat isn't listening – they'll always settle for the 'no-vaccine' option.

I want them to be fit. What can I do?

If your cat isn't into becoming Miss Universe, you might have to make them gym experience more appealing. Cat gyms are well-designed toy combinations, with multiple ledges for cats to clamber onto, swinging toys for them to chase, and surfaces (both vertical and horizontal) for them to scratch. Try sprinkling catnip all over it, or spray it with Feliway, so that it feels more alluring to them. Move it to a different place, out of the line of vision of the window so that stalker cats outside can't eyeball them. Spend time with your cat in the gym, perhaps using a laser pointer to encourage them to run around it. Once they get into the habit, there may be no stopping them.

My cat doesn't want to wear their collar. Do they have to?

They're hooked on a branch with their leg around their head, straining to get away. Such are the dangers of the standard collar. Thank goodness for technology. Now your cat can have an injectable microchip that carries their personal ID and allows exclusive entrance through your home's cat flap. The old bell around the neck is an obvious indication that your cat is 'owned' without the use of a specialized scanner, but listen to them on this one. If it's causing them grief, get them microchipped and let them have their way.

Give them tablets? You must be joking!

The days of the tablet-dodging moggies have been and gone. You can now give worm and flea doses using liquids that are dropped onto the skin. An antibiotic injection is available that lasts for a full two weeks, and a steroid injection can be given that persists for a month. When daily medication is unavoidable, palatable drops that are much more difficult for them to spit out than tablets are often available. If tablets are an absolute must, get some professional pill-giving lessons from the vet. Just don't let your cat see you picking up the towel before you've grabbed them.

About the author

Peter Wedderburn is a vet in a 'companion animal' practice, working only with pets. He has written for many newspapers, including the *Daily Telegraph*, and he regularly contributes to radio and television in the UK and Ireland. He lives in County Wicklow, Ireland, with his wife and two daughters and a menagerie of animals and birds.

His website is www.petethevet.com, and he's on Instagram @Pete.Wedderburn